T0194597

Still! Learning Lessons

HEALING

ARE WE BUILDING WALLS OR CREATING ROOTS?

TRUDI M. WRAY

authorHOUSE®

AuthorHouse™
1663 Liberty Drive
Bloomington, IN 47403
www.authorhouse.com
Phone: 1 (800) 839-8640

Published by AuthorHouse 09/27/2019

ISBN: 978-1-7283-2215-5 (sc)
ISBN: 978-1-7283-2216-2 (hc)
ISBN: 978-1-7283-2217-9 (e)

Library of Congress Control Number: 2019911169

Print information available on the last page.

PREFACE

This book is dedicated to all the "women" who have inspired me through my journey of forgiveness, pain, and love. Each one of you in your own special way has helped me to discover and break down walls of distrust, forgiveness, acceptance and love. Each one of you helped me to establish a strong foundation to grow strong roots for healing. Going through life challenges can be difficult, through my friendship and interaction with some of you I have grown into my wisdom. Sowing the seed within myself to grow roots of understanding and forgiveness toward myself and any situation that may have disappointed or hurt me. What I know for sure through self-discovery, one finds their truest self. The seeds of understanding ignite your spiritual growth, so you can heal and grow into your purpose. This book is dedicated to incredible individuals who I know and whom I do not know. However, what I know for sure is, how much your influence and actions have impacted my life. Through words, positions, professions and friendships. This preface is my way of giving homage to each one of you who has, in some way, shaped my inspirational wisdom in this journey we call life. Some have given me insight in big ways and some in small ways. No matter how these individuals have given me the seed to grow roots and break down walls my heart is full from so many lessons, each one of you have given me. I just wanted to say thank you for empowering me and teaching me so many lessons in the journey we call life. My first thank you, goes to my beautiful mother Dorothy E. Miller and my grandmother Gertrude Hughes, who were the strongest ladies I have ever known. Then, my two incredible daughters who are my inspiration for everything Tiasha Wray, and Jaene' Bindom-Melecio (along with their brothers). To my family and friends who have taught me to love abundantly, forgive with understanding and let go of my ego, thanks you so much; Tiffany Miller, Markita Billups, Patrice Ruttenburg, Freda Miller, Elsie Clark, Minerva Fisher, Rev. Yvonne E. Perry, Myrtle Graham, Herschell Smith, Jackie Queenan, Linda Christian, Sharon Mayes, Selina Braswell, Denise Parnell, Sandy

Mosely, Dr. Beverly Vaughan, Shelly Vazquez, Tosha Lucas, Jackie Irby, Zina Smith, Maku Ali, Sharon-Powell-Lee, Terry Weaver, Lorina Marshall-Blake, Cheryl Matthews, Juanita Mills, Jane Alker, Charita, Marian Edwards, Vicki Curtis, Deborah Harmon-Puge, Taeme Bangura-Pierre, Anali Perez, Jan Lucey, Anna Cordero, Rotita Dandridge, Lisa Risco, Cherita Williams, Margaret Bulter-Williams, Auerlia Saunders, Tamika Thomas, Farah Mabou, Dana McCall, Patty Jackson, Ellen Deitrich, Michelle Williams, Stacey Richard, Susan Heayn, Nekia Hardister, Patrice Jenkins, Penny Bell, Bonnie Seats, Yvonne Deloatch, Shanna Terry, Yvette O Rose, Tiara Harris, Myeshia Gibbons, Kendra Newhart, Samatha Grover, Natalie Orellana, Sharay Tyler and Philece Roberts (*ThatArtista*). The final part of this dedication, I would like to express to all my unknown Sheroes. I dedicated this book to all of you whom I've never had the privilege to know, but have watched from a far the knowledge and empowerment that you demonstrate through the present of storytelling, films, songs, speeches and television. Ladies you energize me for who you are, what you stand for and what you contribute to this world with your grace, passion, courage and commitment. Ladies, I have truly been inspired with your elegances and greatness. I dedicate this book to you as well. Dr. Maya Angelou, Harriett McDaniels, Katherine Hepburn, Audrey Hepburn, Nina Simone, Rachel Maddow, Lena Horne, Hazel Scott, Ella Fitzgerald, Mahalia Jackson, Sarah Vaughan, Diana Ross, Oprah Winfrey, Angela Bassett, Whoopi Goldberg, Viola Davis, Tariji P Henson, Kerry Washington, Angela Davis, Traci Ross, Jada Pinkett-Smith, Ellen DeGeneres, Gwedoyln Brooks, Toni Morrison, Nancy Wilson, Diane Carroll, Eartha Kitt, India Arie, Jill Scott, Queen Latifath, Ledisi, Anita Baker, Toni Baxton, Mary J Beige, Beyonce, Alicia Keys, Betty Shabazz, Coretta Scott King, Duchess of Sussex (Meghan Markle) and First Lady Michelle Obama.

"Let me remind all women that we
live longer and better lives
when we have sisters we love,
not necessarily born in our bloodline or our race".

Dr. Maya Angelou

CONTENTS

Two of my favorite quotes, from
two phenomenal women:
Dr. Maya Angelou and Ms. Oprah Winfrey.

Every time, I step out to achieve
something, I am representing myself
~Dr. Maya Angelou~

When you know who you are, and what
you stand for, you stand in wisdom.
~Ms. Oprah Winfrey~

THE LOVE OF MY MOTHER AND FATHER

*"Loves goes very far beyond the
physical person of the beloved"*
Viktor E Frankel

I've learned the true essence of this statement at a difficult time in my life when I lost my parents within five years of each other. My thoughts were "who is going to love me unconditionally"? My foundation, my absolutes are gone. But what a glorious legacy they gave me to understand I can dream beyond my reach of possibilities and make them a reality. That my destiny, journey and my destination can be more than what I think it can be and to love fully, and to be open, even when you get hurt. Just keep moving and never digress on the hurt or loss, and understand that was a season to learn from and grow into the knowledge of understanding of why this happened, know this too shall pass. As long as you have faith in God because he or she is always on your side and lastly, to embrace your children and grandchildren with the love and understanding that they have no limitation only the ones they place on themselves. Always remember the importance of family. Funny, as I am writing this I remember this saying my father would say from one of Ms. Billie Holiday songs, my father would say, "Gertrude" remember this; Father may have, Mama my have, but God bless the child that has it own. That saying would drive me crazy. I really did not understand or get what he was saying, because he spoiled me so much. After having children, I totally get it, to truly do the best you can for your children is to give them resiliency, have them understand ones self and succeed in their own endeavors, in order to make it in this world. What I've learned from Mr. Frankel, a holocaust survivor and author whose quote is written above, is the essence, I believe, of my parent's spiritual being. Which I realize, is just as important as if my parents were alive. The teachings, strengths and the love they gave me everyday of my life will always stay with me throughout the many seasons of my life. I will keep enduring through my endeavors in this journey toward my purpose in life.

Seeds of faith are always within us;
sometimes it takes a crisis
to nourish and encourage their growth.
-Susan L. Taylor

BLACK BALLED

What one does realized is that when you try to stand up and look the world in the face like you had a right to be here you have attracted the entire power structure of the western world.
~ James Baldwin

I stood up. I went against the power. I was stigmatized and ostracized, for doing what was right, and my punishment was to be labeled a problem, combative, people was told to watch what you say to her, performance is not there. "BLACKBALLED". Because I encountered toxic leadership and I do something about it. I reported it and I became vindicate. The labeling and the undercover reprisal is still going strong, even after I stand for what is right, just and fair even when some people come after the smoke is cleared to give me praise of my actions and commend me for standing up in the midst of the storm when I was standing alone. There was literally a handful of people who stood beside me through this ordeal. The storm was severely heavy at time, causing me to have so many questions, like why did you (God) place me in this position? Was I the voice of reason? Could I stand against the opposition from all levels? Was it I knew my own strength in who I am? Was it, I could and would endure this? Or was it I knew I had the right to be here as well as the right to stand up for what is right and the strength to see it through. What I know for sure in order to stand, one must find the power within. Even when standing alone and going against the power structure. Always rise up to do the right thing, because you know your right and because it's the right and just thing to do, "always".

BARRIERS OF TIME

What I learned about creating barriers, is that you block your blessing for that moment, season or lifetime. People who come into your life are not accidents they were meant to come across your path. However, barriers cause one to be in between life pleasures and moments. It questions the possibilities, it questions whether one should jump or stay on the fence to see a person potential. Instead of embracing the feelings and gut reactions, one feels toward another. Barriers keeps us in a certain situations because we feel it has worked in the past. It becomes a standard behavior. It causes hesitation and doubt and we think time is the answer. The longer we know somebody the easy it is to commit. (So the unconscious mind thinks) Barriers of time are like an erosion. It eats at you one piece at a time. Time is the one thing you cannot get back and barriers of time are baggage, moving into fear from past experiences. With the trust factor as an illusion that is so close, but cannot be reach because feelings and gut reaction are obsolete due to the barriers of time. Barriers of time have no authority of when you feel the way you do toward someone. Barriers of time get in your own way. What I've learned is get out of your own way and just explore the beautiful expressions of new found feelings and see where it will take you. What I've learned for sure about barriers of time is when you go looking for barriers, (such as the good, bad and ugly of someone) one thing is for sure, if you did not find a barrier, you just created a barrier within the other person, because you are searching for the good, the bad, the ugly and that causes barriers. Instead of embracing the moment of life's pleasures, feelings and gut reactions. Once again, the barriers of time just destroyed a possibility.

GOING SOLO

After a fail relationship, which cut at the fiber of
my soul so deeply, I had to do some soul searching,
faith standing, gut-retching, and reality checks to
look at myself, fully. To understand what happened
that ended the relationship and why I got hurt
so badly. As I sat still to recover from my hurt, as
well as to evaluate the cause of what happened, a
couple of things came to mind as I recuperated from
this heart felt breakup. What I learned for sure is
everyone has culpability in a relationship. Second,
if someone cannot love himself or herself, how can
they truly love you (you really cannot change that,
they have to wanted it for themselves). Third, a
quote from one of my favorite writers Maya Angelou
bring this understanding full circle, she stated; "If
we lose love and self respect for each other, this is

how we finally die". I think this is so profound in any relationship, because love and nourishment are key ingredients into growing a relationship. Finally, I realize some people instantly know they are meant for each other, some people are still searching for the right one and some people have the innate concept that they are better off solo. I think I am the latter, so I will go solo and wait on the seeds of faith to bring love, so I can love unconditionally.

GENTLEMEN: (WHERE ARE THEY?)

Being a male is a matter of birth, being a man
is a matter of age. But, being a gentlemen
is a matter of choice. ~Sun-gazing.com

I do not know, how many times I have these thought provoking conversation with my male friends. I am always perplexed of how the male minds works and how they can compartmentalize feelings as well as keep secrets and believe they are keeping it in order to spare feelings. I do not understand how they cannot express their feelings. I do not get it when they say, "I told you the truth", but kept key elements of the situation or relationship out of the explanation. Whatever happened to the gentlemen? Whose actions and words are mirrored, whatever happened to the gentlemen who knows he has a good woman and cherishes her as his Queen? Whatever happened to the gentlemen when nothing can influence your loins because you know what you have at home? Whatever happened to the gentlemen that does and do the right thing because it's the right thing to do. Whatever happened to the gentleman who has the self-respect for himself and the relationship he has. Whatever happened to the gentlemen who open doors and pull out chairs and place the women first in his present, whatever happened to the gentlemen that's let a women know she is the only one in the room for him? What ever happened to the gentlemen who has class, grace, dignity and is respectful of a women worth, instead of explicit language to describe or speak about a women. Whatever happened to the gentlemen that express feelings because he so secure in who he is. Whatever happened to the gentlemen who looks sexy and stylist in a well fitted suit, or casual clothes, whatever happened to a gentlemen who share knowledge and display confidents instead of arrogant? Whatever happened and where are you?

THE TRUTH OF A MAN OR WOMAN

What I've learned about creating walls, when being hurt in a relationship that I believe to be true. A man or woman don't intentionally hurt the one's they love. What I know for sure; a man or women you choose in your life are a representative of who you are. So, if a man or woman hurt you in your life do not start building walls to protect yourself, build an arsenal of understanding of the character traits of that individual. Which I personally call it the "characters tell". (Like poker when a person has a tell or a nervous tick while player cards) It will give yourself a great perspective, and when you see it coming (oh! by the way, you will see it coming) do not build your guard up, instead, re-enforces your negotiable and non negotiable standards that leaves you open instead of being hurt, just say to yourself that this is one of the those non-negotiable standards. I have set for myself and this man or women is not the representative I want in my life.

PURPOSE OF A SOLDIER

One of my greatest penchant for independence and freedom for me is being a soldier in the United States Military. However, being in the military can create a survival mechanism or build walls based on surrounding or environments which you are either order or place in according to duty or mission. Those survival mechanism is more intensified while being on foreign soils. As a soldier I've began to create an intensification (intense + justification) of my ultimate purpose as well as a search for meaning of "why am I a soldier." I've developed this constant need to explore the unknown when I am in unfamiliar territory or situations. This need had me going into a rational investigation of questions in my mind about what is existence, knowledge and ethics are as a soldier. This rational investigation gave me pause for thought about the collection of rules imposed by authority, as a soldier one of my struggle for understanding is "allowing freedom while enforcing order." What I am still learning and trying to create a root of understanding is: "whose freedom are we giving order too"? Is it our domestication of western society that dictates freedom and enforces other culture to embrace our domestication? And if these countries do not embraces our way, then we enforce our western domestication and negate their domestication as well as their cultures of their societies? I do not have the answer to this perplex question, because, it's like peeling an onion. Its, has so many layers with a sprinkle of political brokering. However, what I know for sure "freedom is not free and one's obligations to duty, respect, loyalty, self service and honor is the ultimate sacrifice of dedication, commitment and purpose and that's not free either"…

ONE'S SELF

A Buddhist proverb
There is nothing more dreadful than the habit of
doubt. Doubt separates people. It is a poison that
disintegrates friendship and breaks up relations.

A fellow soldier one day said something to me when
we were on a mission, he called himself the three I's
I am not... I was... I am
A couple of years ago, I was hit with hard times
financially, being broke is when you discover great
friends and friends you thought you were close
too. Borrowing money will test your friendship
and when you cannot pay the money back in the
time allotted back to your friends you will see
who will be standing with you and who will not
be standing with you, even though your reasons

are justified, that you were literally flat broke drowning in debt and needed a life line. Still you are responsible no matter what, even if your game plan falls through. Needless, to say, no matter what some friends want you to find away even try to get blood from a rock, they want their money. Others understand and other know you well enough to know as soon as you get some money they will get paid back and they never talk about it again. So, after much examination of my finances, I tried to explain to my friends, I can pay the money back, it would be over a period of time, due to the game plan falling through. This was my back up to the back up plan. Well! It began, some of my friends call other friends we knew to discuss how I am not this… and I was this…and I am this… I realize to some money is everything and money changes everything for some people. I also realize I have a responsibility to pay my debts and I will pay my debts. What I am still learning through all this is that I was in the middle of three I's, and I place myself in this situations. I could not do what I agreed upon or promise to do.

Disappointments and not paying my debts back on time, I became "**I am not**" a good a friend. I began to be part of the problem complaining how much "**I was**" a good friend, I've always been a good friend, as soon as I had a problem, look how quick some of my friends turn against me, by complaining. I became part of the problem not the solution. Finally, I realize I have made mistake, bit off more than I could handle, made missteps to fulfill a promise. But all in all finances are getting back on track, there is a solid game plan now and I know I am a pretty good friend and a very nice person who had setbacks, challenges, but who has come through and is not done yet.

Because,

"**I am** a work in progress".

TRUTH

*A dog is not considered a good dog because
he is a good barker, a man is not consider a
good man because he is a good talker.
Buddish Proverb….*

What I have learned is that becoming intimate
with someone, is fulfilling, connecting and
embracing. However, just remember, the intimacy
that the two of you are sharing, in that moment
or that season you are also sharing his or her past
intimacies. If you don't understand their history
or their past intimacies your moment or season is
Just consider consenting adults.

*The truth is the only safe ground to stand upon:
"Beyond the lights".*

LAW

What is the law? It is a gun pointed at somebody head it all depends on which end of the gun you're standing to determine whether the law is just or not. Cary Grant... (Talk of the town movie)

As a mother, grandmother, soldier, oh hell! Just a "human being". The ideal conditions of this world should be peace, love and acceptance of everyone. But that's not the case, according to a new book I was reading "The New Jim Crow, written by Michelle Alexander who is an associate professor of law at Ohio State University and holds appointment at the Kirwan Institute for the Study of Race and Ethnicity. Ms. Alexander writes about the Founding fathers of our country who wrote the constitution, it states:

Federalism-the division of power between the states and the federal government-was the device employed to protect the institution of slavery and the political power of slaveholding states. Even the method for determining proportional representation in Congress and identifying the winner of a presidential election (the Electoral College) were specifically developed with interest of slaveholder in mind. Under the terms of our country's founding documents, slaves were defined as three-fifths of a man, not a real, whole human being. Upon this racist fiction rests the entire structure of American democracy.

Democracy, all the sacrifice our ancestors endured, who stood and fought through slavery, jail, bloodshed, assignations and poverty. People of color still rise in believing in this country even though the constitution never acknowledge people of color to be equal. Even though the White House was build on the backs of slaves. Even when the country elected the first African American president, the hate this family endure, but still continue to stay above the fray with grace and dignity, is the bedrock of people of color. As we stood and watch people of color being brutally killed in the streets or being water hose for protecting their land. Their rights as a human being has always been undermined. Even as we witness of a hate filled verbiage throughout a presidential election. Which I was personally, thoroughly confused and disgusted by those behaviors. I find myself asking the question what does the laws of the United States of America stand for? As soon as I wrote those words an "AHA" moment came to me. I completely forgot, it was never a constitutional law for people of color to be equal, therefore, people of color will always be standing at the barrel of a gun pointed at their heads because the law does not recognized people of color as human beings. Therefore, there is no justice for people of color because it sowed into the constitution as so, and everyone knows the constitution is the Law. Unless we improve and change the verbiage in the constitution, now that's a thought.

Abraham Lincoln - America will never be destroyed from the outside. If we falter and lose our freedoms, it well be because we destroyed ourselves.

COMPLETELY

I am not hard to get, all you have to do is ask
"Howard Hawk" writer /director

What I learned, accepting someone into your life as a lover, friend, partner, husband or wife, whatever words are use to describe someone you feel fondly about, is very simple. I don't want to guess where I stand with someone. I do not want half of someone, what I want and expect is the whole person, "completely". I want to be embrace and love for me and I will return those emotions with heart and soul "completely". I cannot be something that I am not and playing a game of in between and not acknowledging and knowing what we mean to each other does not work. So, yes I am hard to get. But, if you are ready and willing, to give me all of you, including your baggage and if you are willing and accepting all my baggage. "Completely"! Then, I am not hard to get, all you have to do is ask me.

TONGUE

The tongue, like a sharp knife kills
without drawing blood.
-Unknown-

What I have learned, seems a lifetime ago, I was
told, "who is going to want you with three kids."
That conversation to this day still resonate with me,
not like it used to, back then it cause insecurity as
a women, who had children and was alone, trying
to take care of herself and her children on her own.
The truth is, I believed, I failed, for myself and for
my children, I realized, I had to restart my life.
First step, was moving back in with my mother.
Me and my children were sleeping on my mother
living floor. (Thank God, I had a strong mother)
because she instill in me strength, as well as always

being there for your children. I realized, while I was putting my life back together. People will date you with three children, you have to believe in yourself, have a drive and know your worth to overcome labels. They will admire you for you resiliency to remove yourself and your children from toxic situation and finally, I believe the bedrock for me, is as long as you have respect, love, loyalty and togetherness, you are at peace. Yes! The tongue is sharp, something's said from the mouth will never be forgotten. However, as Martin Luther King Jr. once said and is true "A man can't ride your back unless it bent." I chose to stand tall, not break, and definitely not bend on any toxic environments.

WAITING

Hope never rest in man
Bible (KJV)

I decide some time ago (I am not going to tell you how long) to sit still and take care of my space, myself, to observe introspectively what my purpose is and what I really want in my life as far as a relationship. This is an interesting process, because if you can get comfortable sitting still and being alone, you will know the one you are choosing is out of love and not out of loneliness. I thought this was crazy for me to do, but it works, you can see clearly what is coming at you and if you remove sex from the equation, you will see people true nature, sitting still gives discernment to see the true nature of a person. I have fell into pitfalls of not waiting and jumping in based on words instead of actions and if their actions did not mirrored together with their words. I would try to fix it because I invested so much time in the relationship instead of getting out of it, or learning from it. God knows, I have experience what I did not want in a relationship and I have paid some cost in choosing those selective relationships. What I have learned is a couple of things, when someone shows you who they really are believe them, when someone you love say they love you but the actions show something different, you should be leaving and not trying to fix it. Also, remember this, the beginning of an affair starts with a conversation, so I suggest upgrade, be choosey from what you have learned, sit still and wait for what you want, because your happiness, hopes and dream rest with in you.

LONELY CHILD

There is no greater agony than bearing
an untold story inside you.
Maya Angelou~

What I am learning is how to heal. I have so many emotions trying to write this, I was born into a family with a total of eight siblings, me being the youngest sibling, I was the baby, with a twenty year age gap between six of my siblings. Needless to say, even though I had seven older sibling, I felt I was a lonely child. This situation has migrated into my adulthood. There are so many heart wrenching events I have experience through my childhood. One event I remember so vividly when it came time to go on a family trip to go to Wildwood, NJ. I was left at home, I had a mother and a father the rest of my siblings only had my mother. Because of this difference, I was ostracized, so they drove off, leaving me behind.

Wow! Still stings. The funny thing is, I don't remember my mother ever correcting this behavior. I do not know when it started but my feelings of loneliness came extremely early for me. It's not until adulthood when I started realizing somethings that was said were not truthful. But the damage was already done. Reminiscing about these stories, I remember trying to heal, during my mother's home going. I promised my mother I would try. I would let go of my distrust and hurt. I tried, but when I learned about the placement of cement for mother's headstone as well as not being a part of the ceremony for mother's headstone. It brought up a laundry list of so many things. I could not forget, so I do not engage in any conversation with my family members. What I am learning now, is my childhood made me struggle with acceptance and cause me to accept crumbles of love until I had my own children. Unconditional love and acceptance as a mom, is a wonderful and joyous feeling knowing that my children accepts me unconditionally, loves me and is proud that I am their mother, means everything. Hopefully, I have succeeded with my children, as well as to show togetherness and having each other back through thick and thin. It's my hope that they understand why that is so important to me, because I never experience that feeling until I experience it with them.

~God bless Motherhood~

WHY?

The best thing about the past is that it shows you what not to bring to the future. "Unknown"

Why did I feel I was a lonely young child?

Why as a little girl did I have to witness individuals disrespect my father, and then years later, ask him for financial help which they never repaid?

Why as a young child did I experience so much divisiveness with choosing to believe one over the other without getting the full story?

Why was there a belief I had more?

Why after moving in with my mother, and mother gave me the house, a meeting is held to see how the house can be obtain.

Why was I so misunderstood and gossiped about?

Why would there be a celebration of mother's headstone and I was not notified or invited?

Why was I so hopeful and excited of being acknowledge and wanting that validation so much, why did I need it?

Why did I feel I was not good enough or deserving to be loved unconditionally?

Why was there no support toward me when my father died?

Why do I place barriers around me and not associate with family, and feel fine with that?

Why?

I AM ENOUGH

*Happiness is from within it is not a matter
of externals- Abraham Lincoln*

My patience has been tested too many times.
My time can no longer be wasted. My
disappointment of people hurting me has to be
brushed off and leave it outside of my home.
My will of always trying to fix' and please no
longer exist. My flexibility of compromise and
understanding through betrayal, dishonesty and the
lack of common decency and respect is completely
cut off once it is shown to me. My acceptance of
behavior from friends who do not know how to give
encouragement or a compliment is negative and
please understand negativity is unacceptable to me.

Finally!

My embracement of myself as well
as allowing myself to be happy and
enjoying my purpose in life, says,
I am enough.

TRUDI'S MANTRA

One of those life moment, I actually had the distinct pleasure of reaching out to Mr. Jose Micard Teixeira and I asked him could I use his poem "I no longer" when I first read his poem I had just completed something I wrote called "I am enough". Mr Teixeira, poem resonated with me so powerfully, I read it, every day, and it's on my wall at my office and my home. It truly is my Mantra, it speak to who I am and when Mr. Teixeira replied back and said: yes. I could use his quote that was so awesome, so here is Trudi's mantra with permission from Mr. Jose Micard Teixeira, Thank you!

"I no longer have patience for certain things, not because I've become arrogant, but simply because I reached a point in my life where I do not want to

waste more time with what displeases me or hurts me. I have no patience for cynicism, excessive criticism and demands of any nature. I lost the will to please those who do not like me, to love those who do not love me and to smile at those who do not want to smile at me. I no longer spend a single minute on those who lie or want to manipulate. I decide not to coexist anymore with pretense, hypocrisy, dishonesty and cheap praise.

I do not tolerate selective erudition nor academic arrogance. I do not adjust either to popular gossiping. I hate conflict and comparisons. I believe in a world of opposites and that's why I avoid people with rigid and inflexible personalities. In friendship I dislike the lack of loyalty and betrayal. I do not get along with those who do not know how to give a compliment or a word of encouragement. Exaggerations bore me and I have difficulty accepting those who do not like animals. And on top of everything I have no patience for anyone who does not deserve my patience."

~Mr. Jose`Micard Teixeira~

TALK

No person is your friend who demands your silence, or denies your right to grow.
~Alice Walker

There was a time when my words seem to be deaf to the ear, my voice at times was muffled in order to keep peace. The uncertainty within myself as a young girl was why talk when you do not hear me or listen to my feelings. So I've learned as a child to go inside myself, to create a world that fantasied the strength of a women. I started embracing the old movies 20's, 30's and 40's which depicted strong women in major roles such as Lena Horne, Katherine Hepburn, Barbara Stanwyck, Ginger Rogers, Bette Davis, Joan Crawford, the list can go on and on. I started creating a world of what I expected and thought of myself and learned to grow into that manifestation of that person. A true renaissance woman. Through old movies and the way the writers showed love, glamor, respect and the wit of the English word to express without degrading or using obscene language to get a point across. Wow! within that moments, a hour or hour and forty-five minutes had passed by, my cup was running over, I was full, to embrace life challenges, I was ready, to be out front with no hesitation, my silence became my empowerment, my rights as human being, young lady, and a woman! Would never be denied or in a shadow of being quite ever again. I learned from these movies how to love myself authentically,

OTHER SIDE

Pedestals-sometimes people put people on pedestals so they can see them more clearly and knock them off more easily~ Maya Angelou

One day I ran into someone I have known for twenty plus years, I believed he had everything going for him, authentic in himself, great career, integrity, character of what I knew about him.

I really could not understand why we did not work out, feeling he is the one that got away. The pedestals, I place this person on was enormous.

I asked God, a question why not me? Why couldn't you have given somewhat like this to me? I am a really nice person deserving to be appreciated, respected and enjoy this abundant life he seems to have carved out for himself. As soon as I spoke these words, God has a way of showing you why this was not for you. Once you see the flaws of unhappiness and realize the mentality is cheaper to keep because of position and power and seeing up close and personal, the unhappiness and not living their authentic truth. The characteristic and integrity I once thought was there, made me question, did I just see what I wanted to see? So no more pedestals, because the other side is just another side of a human being.

BEING ME!

One of the hardest things I ever had to learn is to come back into the light of my purpose. To understand why the darkness of the pain and dealing with the games of deceit was so draining on my mind and body. I did not have the energy to explore any type of relationship. I had to focus on being me again. What I know, about being me is, when I like you, I like you. When I love you, I love you, nothing in between. I give my all, maybe too much at times, that I lose my self, because I gave my thought process the acknowledgement that this was being me, my authentic self. I have to give everything, totally and unconditionally. However, I realize I can continue to be me, with the understanding, some only want what they want and some people mean you no good and that no one except your spiritual belief (God, Jehovah,

Yahweh whatever you call your spiritual belief) should be your "everything" in your life. So, I've learned going forward, my spiritual belief will be the only one to occupy my "everything" space. I will continue to be me, standing in my light and purpose to empower, love and give myself with openness and truth, with a little caveat that my "everything" space is for my spiritual belief and no human being will own or occupy that space because, its simply not healthy too.

STRENGTH

They see me as a threat of some kind, every strong woman in history had to walk down this similar path it's the strength that causes the confusion and fear. ~Princess Diana

WHAT! is it the arch in my back you do not understand, is it I know more than I say, is it I think more than I speak or is it I notice more than you realize. **WHY?** Is my strength such a threat, why is my strength subject to labeling me as being aggressive, pushy, know it all. **BY!** Whose authority does anyone has the right to undermine my strength in order to feel adequate with in them. **MY!** Strength is earned and will not be comprised, because you do not understand the strong arch in my present when I walk into a room or understand my struggles in this journey we call life. Since you have no clue, **THEN!** Just stop with the labeling and instead support it, except it and learn from it. PERIOD!

COMFORT ZONE

How they treat you is how they feel about you. Period! ~Simple Reminder.com

Several friends told me to step out of my comfort zone because they wanted to see me happy. I could not fathom of stepping out of what I believe my ideals desire for me was, or give up what my expectation are for someone to come and be in my life. I did not care how long I would have to wait for this ideal relationship. However, life is not like that, life is much funnier. Being open allows a moment, season or lifetime to touch your space. It is vital for human connection, to be able to embrace that intimacy, it is truly amazing. I honestly lost that feeling, it was an empty space for a long time, and I could not remember those feelings because I locked them away so I would not be hurt again. I realized, through my beautiful friends I needed to exist again and not sit on the sideline and just imagine what and if about an ideal relationship. I met someone who is funny, younger and make me laugh and he realized I am green in some areas, but he truly gets me for me. I realized in that moment I was not growing and I had to step out of my comfort zone and step into a moment, season or maybe a lifetime. When I totally got out of my own way and realize that I should never underestimate the power of a connection no matter the age and embrace whatever is happening, I found the truest lesson learned is to stay open and prepare your heart for whatever comes and that every relationship is a lesson...

SOME PEOPLE

Never allow yourself to be define by
someone's else opinion of you
~ SimpleReminder.com

Some people will write you off without ever knowing you, they feed off of what they heard about you. Some people judge and feed off of gossip. Some people will not apologize when they're wrong. Some people will judge you on your choices you make, when they do not even know the options you had to choose from. Some people, will judge you and never have walked in your shoes to know if they fit or are a little too tight. Some people minds will always feed on the negativity when reality is staring them in the face. Some people can and will dislike you for absolutely no reason at all. It's really easy to give in to the pressure of knowing some people dislike you for one reason or another, it's easy for fear to slip through and question why me? What have I done that this person does not like me. However, I noticed I still endure and persevere, and realize I am not interested in some people's perception of me. I am wiser and stronger in my walk of being my authentic self and I frankly do not give a DAMN about what some people think.

POWER

*When the Power of Love, overcome the Love
of Power the world will know peace.*
~Jimi Hendrix

There are standard within the military branches which everyone is supposed to be measures by throughout their entire military career. These standards are extremely powerful they are inclusive in the daily life of military service, they are: loyalty, duty, respect, honor, integrity, personal courage and selfless-service. These powerful depictions of character traits judge and mold opinion of every military personnel. The military uses these standards to judge your compatibilities and leadership within the military, with that said when you come up against senior leadership not leading by example and you go against the grain and standup with every fiber in your being to do what rights in that process you are ostracized. When you initiate an action or report that represents a correction to those standards you are label difficult. Finally, the other side of power rears its ugly head within the military ranks to protect an imaginary standard for some leader in order for them not to become exposed. It's called reprisal, reprisal is whispering throughout the unit or command to destroy the creditability, character, performance and the integrity of the military person who stood up for what was right and just. When stepping up to toxic leadership and acting on that injustice toward military personnel as well as try and uphold the standard we hold true, you are a target and you are in the cross hair. Any challenges of growth within yourself as a soldier becomes the talk between mid and senior leadership. Reprisal is meant to understand the power of rank not obligation, and with increase rank comes great power and with that power it is a belief and a mindset that if high ranking official is not asking you, to do something illegal, ill moral or unethical. Then everything is proper. This is ingrain in the tradition of military life. However it simply not true, somethings are not proper because it is permissible nor is it ethical because it does not violate legal or ethical standards. The standard we measure should be a higher caliber as a soldier. The power of love for the tradition of service and integrity is a beautiful and fulfilling experience with in the military. However, if you truly believe and live by all the inclusive standards you will surely go against the power of rank and encounter reprisal. What I have learned for sure is you must justified your existence when you stand up and speak the truth even though you know you are going be ostracized, stand on a platform of doing what is right and fair no matter what the rank is. By doing this, the love of power, will meet and greet the power of love for military standards and in turn the caliber at the highest degree would be establish for that soldier/soldiers as they will be recognize as always doing what is right and what is just. HOOAH!

PERSEVERANCE

Take chances, make mistake, that's how you grow, pain nourish your courage, you have to fail in order to practice being brave ~ Mary Tyler Moore

I have failed more times than I can count. My motto from a single mother perspective, was for my children, not to see how hard the struggle was for me to make ends meet. I used the term in my head all the time, "fake it until you make it" or "we make it do what we got to do". I was literally juggling bills in order to accomplish a graduation or a move to college dorm. I was literally counting from my penny jar, trying to figure out gas money to get there and gas money to get home. I was doing everything, working part-time jobs, cleaning bathrooms and questioning all the time how do I have all this education and I am still living paycheck to paycheck. There was so many times I was living out of my means due to pride of doing it alone and pride to not let my children feel they were living in single parent home. Hindsight is twenty –twenty looking back that was not a good thing to do, it created debt and it shelters my children to think they lived a life of privilege or a privilege life. What I've learned no matter the education or life experiences which one may achieve, life is what you make out of it, you have to ride life not let life ride you. During failed times, you have to fall forward to pick yourself up and understand effort does not guarantee outcome. What failure and effort does say is that you have the perseverance to take a chance, to grow in your resiliency and be empower to move pass mistake, failure, and financial hardship. The power of perseverance within oneself assures you that you will not break due to setback and miss opportunities, and that you will grow in your nourishment of mistakes and failures, and that you will be encourage through this journey of life to keep moving and never stop persevering through any endeavors alone the way.

AGE

Despite how open, peaceful, and loving you attempt to be, people can only meet you as deeply as they're met themselves ~ Unknown

What I have learned, age is nothing but a number. It is not by age, but, by knowledge is how wisdom is acquired. Also, I have learned, how you see yourself, can be a reflection with who you are with and that can deeply divide the age difference significantly. Despite, how much you care for someone, if you don't see them growing in knowledge, or matters of wisdom at the age they are representing, then the confirmation has been delivered in the flesh. For you to understand that everybody cannot come with you in your growth to the next level of your journey. Age and wisdom you would think should go hand and hand, but it does not, sometimes, the age surpass the wisdom based on time.

The life we choose and the environment that we want to surround ourselves with, may not be the environment we may have been expose to as child or young adult. As you age, wisdom is more real and tangible, you finally understand what you need, what you will accept and what you will not accept. Age, has a way of showing throughout the years the transformation of growth and knowledge of lessons learned within yourself. No longer are you worried about how and when you should, show affection or expressions of love to someone. No longer are you afraid to embrace what you feel because you know life is too short for anything else. However, be sure that the age of maturity is evenly yoke, that it is in sync with your ideals of expression, because if they are not in sync, then it isn't worth having and age is not just a number anymore. It's a piece of time, you given freely and the other person was not worthy of that expression or time. What I have learned and received from this lesson is that people can only meet you where their maturity and growth are at. Time and age is not only a number it shows you the reflection of your choices. The age differences for both in that moment truly shows you are still learning wisdom.

PEOPLE

What I've learned about most people, they don't have a problem of seeing what is right or wrong the problem comes when it time to do the right thing. Unknown

Struggling with the bullshit of people, being a parent whether through a marriage, boyfriend and girlfriend, unplanned, one night stand or even if you dislike the person, carrying the baby or who planted the seed for you to carry this gift, the thought of not doing what is right for the child/children is "BULLSHIT". The bottom line, the child is an innocent person in this equation. That moment of fulfillment while in the act of conceiving this gift, should be enough for you to see and nurture the growth of this little gift. The bullshit should not be: I am not doing anything because of garnishes wages, or not having an active role in the child life because you don't like the father or the mother, or not contributing finances because you think the mother or father is spending all the money. The solutions should not be waiting until you see your child/children graduate from school/college to be the proud parent, while basting in that glorious milestone, you stand arrogantly proud flexing your muscle like you contribute and nurture that growth, when you never gave a concern of when they had to be rush to the hospital, or up all night with them through fevers or upset stomach or when they are late coming home, or first time driving, or first steps into becoming a young lady or a young man, or their first serious relationship. No! Instead of witnessing these milestone, that sacrifice of giving was not in your DNA, but the bullshit of cynicism and criticism to the other parent who sacrifice to be in the present of their child/children to make sure they were love and nurture, is a way, to not look at your own shortcomings. Being a single parent can be at times a thankless job, because the child/children knows and take for grant that the single parent who nurture them through everything is not going anywhere, they know you will be there for them. But somehow the one parent who was not there, who self —preservation was only paramount to themselves and for themselves, it seems the child/children are always in a need to be accepted and approve by them, and after all the hard work is done there is a re-appearance, and a willingness to get to know the child/children and accept the pretense and hypocrisy that they actually did so much when in reality they did nothing, nor acknowledge and appreciate what the other parent sacrifice to accomplish with their child/children. It can be extremely difficult to take, while smiling and accepting their bullshit, for your child/children sake, when you know the right thing was not done in the first place.

GRATITUDE

*Missteps in life has made me the woman
I am today grateful ~* Trudi Wray

What I have learned for sure is every mistake, slip-up, blunders, errors, bloopers, lapse, fault, inaccuracies, oversight, shortcomings, indiscretions, miscalculations. I own it, because without these missteps I truly would not understand how to get out of my own way and run into my purpose. I would not know how to let things go and not look at those situations as wasted time, but instead, learned lesson. Without the errors I would not have the power of discernment to now see the parasites as they come. Because of miscalculation, I now see the different between two types of friendship one was monetary based and the other is a genuine friendship that stands with you while it's raining and still is your friend despite your shortcomings. Without the lapse in judgments of men, I would not have experience the greatest joy of giving birth to my beautiful children. Without the mistakes of trying to over compensate for my children, because my pride never wanted them to ever feel slighted that they were being raised by a single parent. I now understand the financial responsibility that incurs with that decision as well as the blunders and bloopers of trying to overcome those financial responsibilities. Without the indiscretions, I now understand and know my worth and what is negotiable and non-negotiable for me in a relationship. Without the inaccuracies of my thinking that I am the mother so I am right, on raising sons and not looking at my own faults and slips-up I would not have learned, when raising sons, I can give them the tools to be respectful, hardworking and kind. However, I could not equip them on how to be a man, that's a fault, I completely own. Because I had no oversight to introduce them to positive male present in their life. I felt they were my responsibility and my pride said I would teach them everything they need to know. I would not rely on anyone to help me with my children except my mother. I've learned some hard mistakes on this one. Through all my missteps, it has help me to keep the faith, stay focus, get back up and keep moving, forward through my journey to find my authentic and truest self and enjoy the lessons learned in this journey toward fulfillment and happiness.

Which I am profoundly grateful. ~ Trudi

QUESTION: WHEN WAS IT OK?

Insulted me, cheated on me, beat on me, robbed me, those who are free of resentful thoughts surely will find peace -unknown

What I learned for sure is a person who goes through abuse, whether it is physical or mental abuse, they are formed and molded by those thoughts and in order to move on and live peacefully, there will be a time when you ask yourself questions. When was it ok? The questions may never be answer, however find comfort and peace that you are not alone and never digress (backward) only progress (forward). Remember Karma! (Asking a lot of question is one way to get answers)

1. When was it ok? To not take care of your responsibility as a father/mother?

2. When was it ok? To show your child/children they are not first in your life?

3. When was it ok? That selfishness was the only requirement for parenthood, marriage or a relationship?

4. When was it ok? To try and control another person?

5. When was it ok? To constantly take and feed nothing to the soul?

6. When was it ok? To have two different families at the same time?

7. When was it ok? To meet and cheat with someone you barely knew?

8. When was it ok? To write letters to another women/man?

9. When was it ok? To think and try to place your hands on someone?

10. When was it ok? To play mental games of moving and returning items back as though they were never lost?

11. When was it ok? To insult a person because they decided to leave you?

12. When was it ok? To not respect the sanctity of marriage?

13. When was it ok? To lie and misrepresent yourself because you want what you want no matter the cost?

14. When was it ok? To give someone a STD because you cheated?

15. When was it ok? To neglect a child/children because you don't like the other parent?

Please tell us
WHEN WAS IT OK?

EDUCATION

Education is the passport to the future, for tomorrow belongs to those who prepare for it today ~ Malcolm X

There is a saying "most opportunities are missed because most people like things that come easy." Some people think, to put effort and work for something can be too hard to do when things have always came easy for them. Some people believe, putting effort in to something when it does not come easy is not fulfilling. Some people do not see the reward of the accomplishments or understand if they just gave a little more effort, the opportunities would be abundant. So, miss opportunities, creates limitation of choices. This was a harsh reality, when it hits close to home, no matter what you want for your children, you cannot drag them across the finish line to complete a degree or choose the right partner for them. The opportunities provided, does not mean that is the choice they wanted or is going to choose. When they have so many distraction in their lives. Education is the passport to the future, how that education is obtain is the question. Through formal education or life choices, either way, you are going to learn a lesson. What I learned about the journey of education is no one can draw a road map on how you get this education. Even though, you may want too. Learning to let go and release your expectation is the first step in allowing them to understand and determine, what was a miss opportunities for them as they are watching on the sideline, as their future passport is passing them by. Therefore realizing their preparations for tomorrows was a miss opportunity and now they only have a pipe dream or a realization that they must create a passport by getting up and get moving toward their future so their tomorrows can begin.

INTESTINAL FORTITUDE

*Defining fair is based on the person who
is judging the fairness-unknown*

What I have learned, it is time to retire from the
U.S. Military, fairness is truly based on who is
judging and ego is always at the forefront. Efforts,
does not guarantee outcome and support, is a
system that only worth what it cost you to give
it. The military has become a business. Not too
many people speak truth to power. When you
speak the truth and justified your existence in
this organization for what is right and you share
the light of truth and not just go with flow of
things, you are a target. The band wagon begin
to circle you and you become a threat. Intestinal
fortitude become your mantra, your goal

To reach the 20 year mark to obtain a pension, use the GI Bill to obtain formal educational training to obtain a degree or maybe a couple of degrees and just go with the flow until you reach that landmark. I know this to be so, because this business has helped me and my family. However, acceptance of mediocrity, unacceptable. I am proud to say throughout my military career. I have stood up to toxic power, went to Inspector General on toxic power. I have never tolerate mediocrity in my military career, this has gotten me in a lot of situations. However, if you do what is right, you can never be wrong and that's because of intestinal fortitude

TANGLED WEB

When deceit is the daily practices toward someone you are supposed to be in love with, the only outcome will always be a tangle web. ~unknown

One day, I ran into an ex-relationship, nobody could not tell me this person was not the one. (Except for my daughter instinct). We did all the pleasantries, how is the family etc. I heard you got marriage and have a child, he replied he did and his stated the child age. I said Oh! Really, well congratulations and take care. I walked away, saying to myself, I guess you never calculated that it was the same time we broke up. Hum!

Tangled web

BOTHER ME

Never chase love, affection or attention,
if it isn't given freely by another person,
it isn't worth having- unknown

Everything leads from the heart, I want somebody to bother me to the point they intoxicate my soul with their eyes. I want to experience ground shaking, life altering, knock you on your ass feelings. I want consistency, love abundantly, ride or die loyalty, someone to fight for me, adore me and love me unconditionally. So bother me.

Because!

I AM A QUEEN

FATHER'S PERSPECTIVE

*The sparkle depends on the flaw in
the diamond ~unknown*

My dad was a man of few words, but his insight into people was incredible. His instinct was absolute. My dad would always say, "I am a diamond in the rough". I always thought this was a backwards compliment and never truly listened to him. I was always looking for validation of who I was, due to the experiences in my childhood and marriage. If I just understood my dad's communication style, my conflict and peace of mind would have been resolved a long time ago. The tears I cried before they fell would not have created an indelible portrait of wanting to be accepted. Instead, I would have known I was already authentic. A one of kind genuine gem and all I needed was to be polished.

CHILDREN

Something just exist to be beautiful- unknown

My children and grandchildren just exist to be beautiful. I am so blessed that God has chosen me to be their mom and GG for my grandchildren. They are truly my air. What I am learning is to relax, release and let go. My children have their own directions, it may not be, what I would have chosen or wished for, however it is their path. They have chosen for themselves. As a single mom, doing everything when they were young, I was in control and now that they are adults, learning my place in this evolution of adulthood is like walking on a tight rope. It is much harder than I thought. I want to fix everything, I want to be heard, and I want to be direct. I want that control to fix things as I would do when they were young. I cannot do that anymore. I have to let go and let them run to their own destiny. I have to put my feelings in check, so I don't feel hurt if they forget something I ask them to do, or feel forgotten because their priorities in life does not place me first. The line of succession changes as you grow. Who would come first as child is not the same as who comes first when you are an adult. That does not mean you are not an important part of their lives, you are just not immediate. That is circle of life, that's the way it goes with having their own families. I was the heavy who lies at the head, when they were young, no longer is that my role. Now, going forward, I am learning to let go and enjoy my empty nest.

AUTHORS PAGE

"Healing is a book about overcoming and speaking out loud, what has ran through my mind during life experiences. Writing "Healing" I can see my transformation, it has forced me thoroughly, to look at my missteps, harsh realities of acceptance and empowerment to become my authentic self. It also showed me that I am still a work in progress, because somethings in my life experience still stings and I have not truly gotten over it. Forgiveness is the key and I am learning to forgive myself, but I realize I will never forget. So, I am embracing my healing process to become my authentic self. I like who I am, I appreciate who I am, and I respect who I am, going forward with the rest of my life I will not accept anything less, because I am grateful.

ABOUT THE AUTHOR

This is Trudi M. Wray's second book, her first book "Still Learning Lesson Even after Forty" was the beginning of trying to understand her perspective of what she was feeling inside. Trudi's second book explain these emotions with intestinal fortitude. Trudi has revealed some heartfelt, life changing moments in her quest to embrace her heartache, missteps in life to become her authentic self. Trudi M. Wray holds a dual Bachelor Degree, Master degree, and working towards finishing her PhD program. She is a mother of four beautiful children and have seven amazing grandchildren. She lives a quiet life while enjoying and living her truest self.

Printed in the United States
By Bookmasters